This workbook belon

C000064349

Hello 你好 nǐ hǎo

This workbook will introduce you and your child to the common basic and compound strokes used in writing Chinese characters.

Practice writing strokes with pre-writing exercises. Recognize and color Chinese words. Trace Chinese characters by following stroke order diagrams.

How to Trace:
Trace over the gray characters by following the correct numbered stroke order as shown for the first few grids. Do not worry about the thickness of the gray lines. Use a pencil or pen to trace down the middle of the gray lines. Practice with this sample grid.

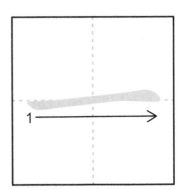

Thank you for choosing **Chinese For Kids First Practice Strokes Ages 4+ (Simplified)**. This workbook is best used with pens, pencils, colored pencils and crayons. Have fun writing and learning!

Chinese For Kids First Practice Strokes Ages 4+ (Simplified)
Copyright 2019 Queenie Law
Adore Neko Designs
www.adoreneko.com
ISBN: 9781797428970

Table of Contents

Basic Strokes

Compound Strokes

Table of Contents

Chinese Characters

 diǎn

左 点

left dot
zuǒ diǎn

 Use your finger to trace the zuǒ diǎn.

✏️ Use a pencil to trace each zuǒ diǎn ◗ .

1

diǎn

字

WORD

word
zì

✏️ Use a pencil to trace each zuǒ diǎn ◗ .

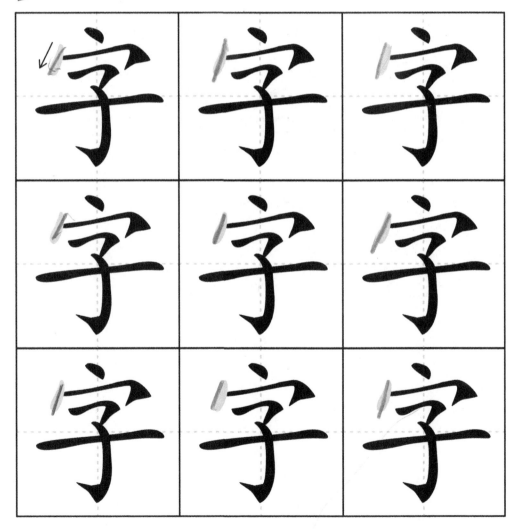

2

 diǎn

右点

right dot
yòu diǎn

👆 Use your finger to trace the yòu diǎn.

✏️ Use a pencil to trace each yòu diǎn .

3

diǎn

头

head
tóu

Use a pencil to trace each yòu diǎn ●.

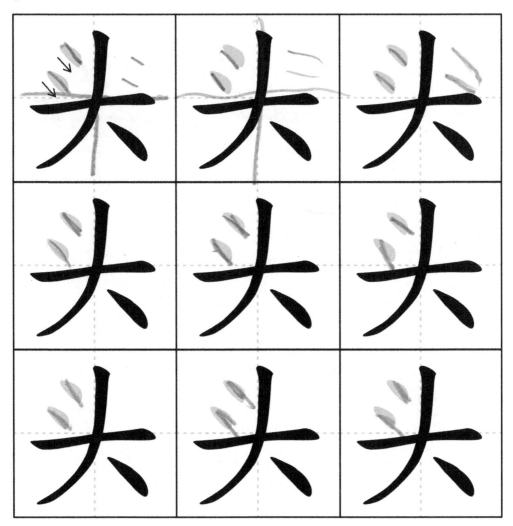

 héng

短横

short horizontal
duǎn héng

 Use your finger to trace each **duǎn héng**.

 Trace each **duǎn héng** ━ .

5

héng

two
èr

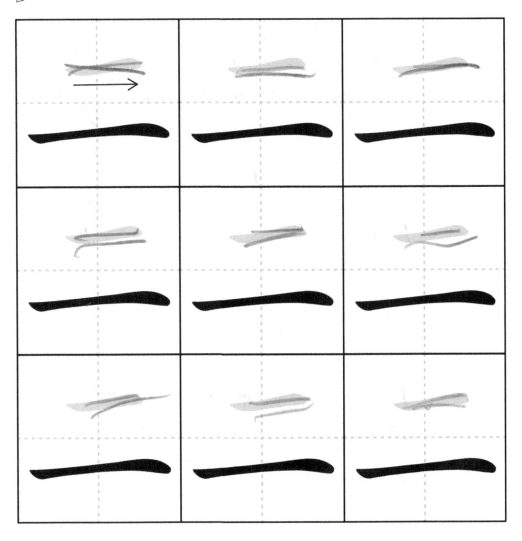

✏️ Use a pencil to trace each duǎn héng ➍.

 héng

长横

long horizontal
cháng héng

 Use your finger to trace each cháng héng.

 Use a pencil to trace each cháng héng ——.

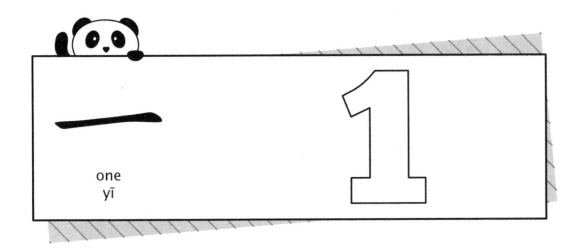

一

one
yī

1

✏ Use a pencil to trace each cháng héng ━ .

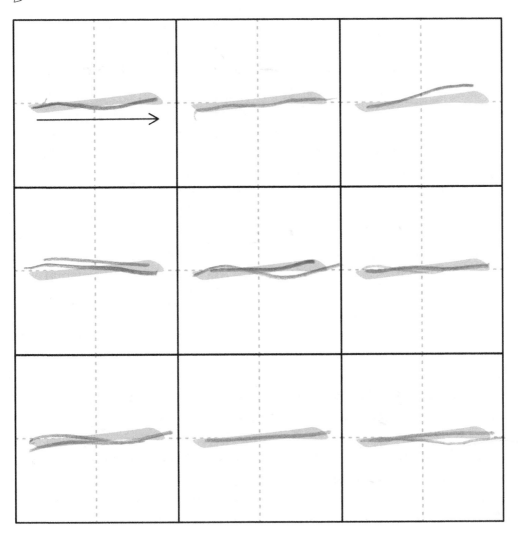

 shù

短竖

short vertical
duǎn shù

 Use your finger to trace the duǎn shù.

Use a pencil to trace each duǎn shù ▎.

9

shù

工

work
gōng

 Use a pencil to trace each duǎn shù **❘**.

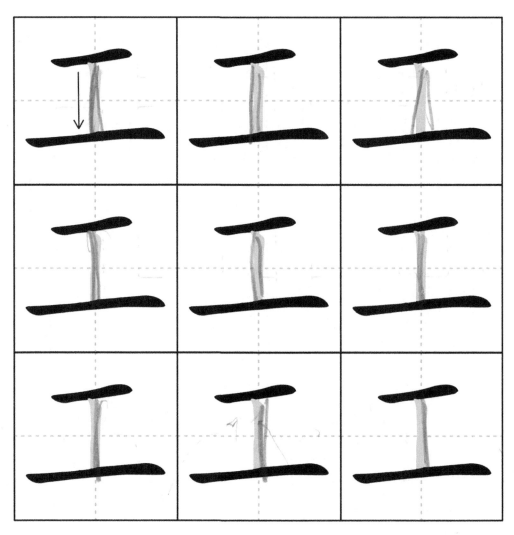

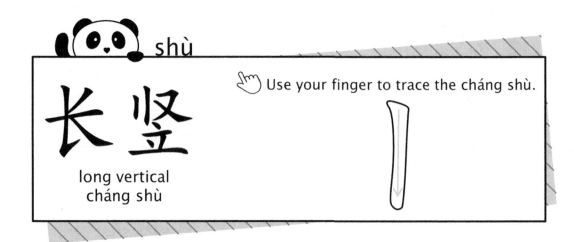

shù

长竖

long vertical
cháng shù

Use your finger to trace the cháng shù.

Use a pencil to trace each cháng shù |.

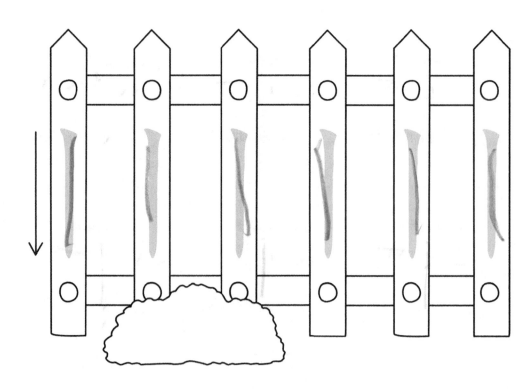

shù

十

ten
shí

 Use a pencil to trace each cháng shù 丨.

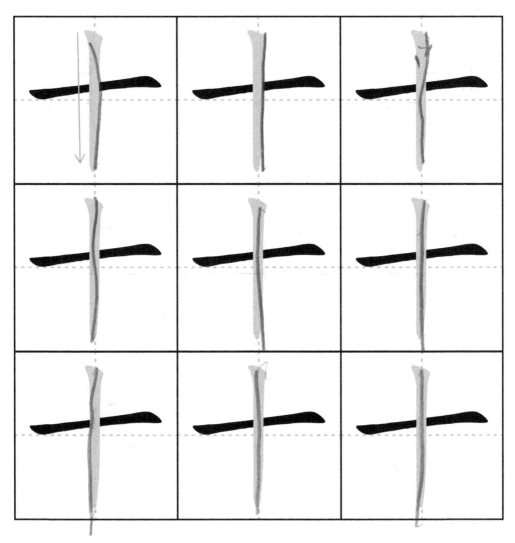

长撇

long falling
cháng piě

Use your finger to trace the cháng piě.

Use a pencil to trace each cháng piě ノ.

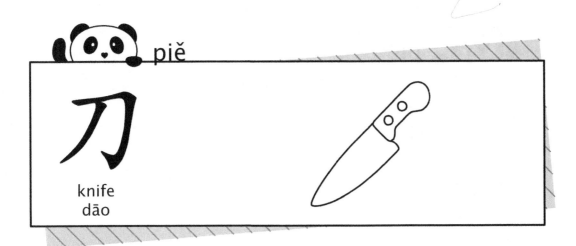

piě

刀

knife
dāo

✏️ Use a pencil to trace each cháng piě ㇓.

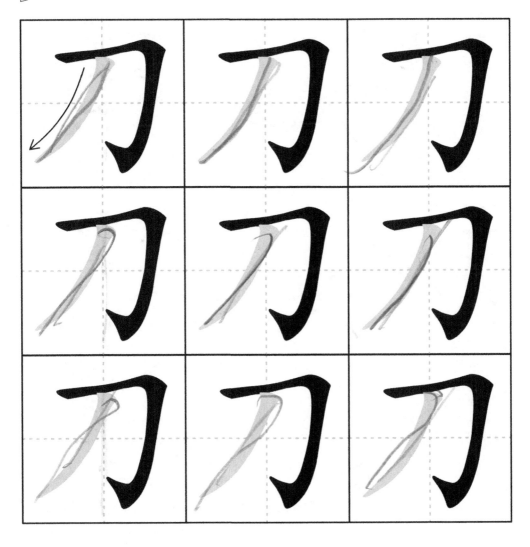

 **piě**

短撇

short falling
duǎn piě

🖑 Use your finger to trace the duǎn piě.

✏️ Use a pencil to trace each duǎn piě ノ.

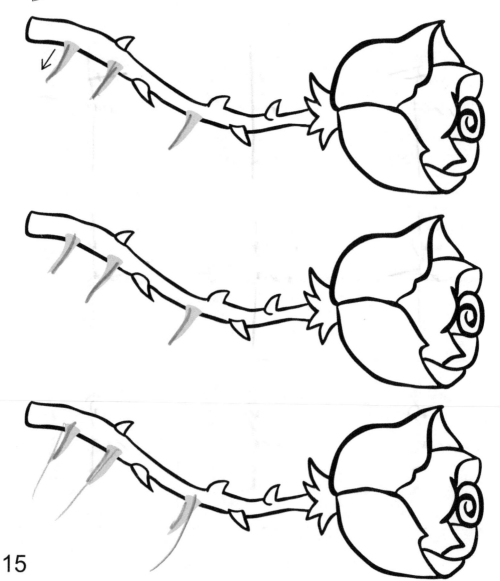

15

牛

cow
niú

✏️ Use a pencil to trace each duǎn piě ✓.

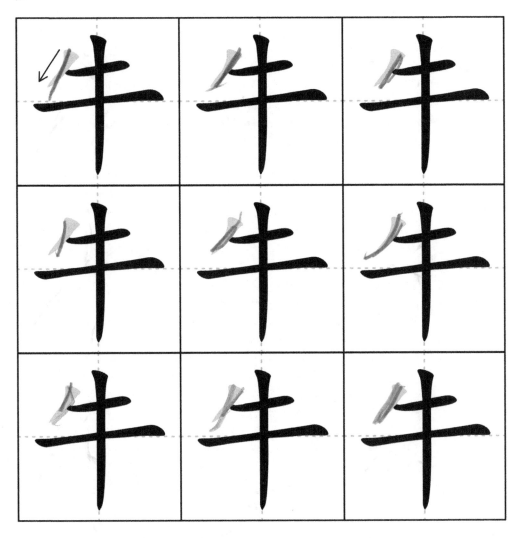

 piě

平撇

flat falling
píng piě

Use your finger to trace the píng piě.

Use a pencil to trace each píng piě ◣.

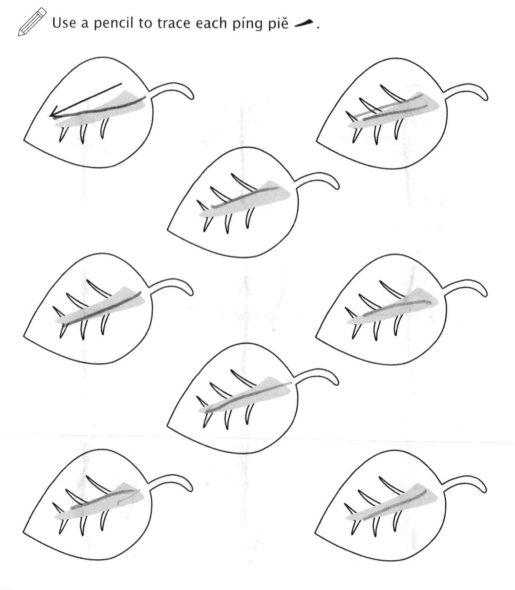

17

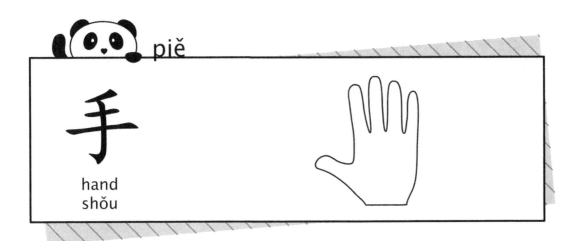

piě

手

hand
shǒu

✏ Use a pencil to trace each píng piě ⌐ .

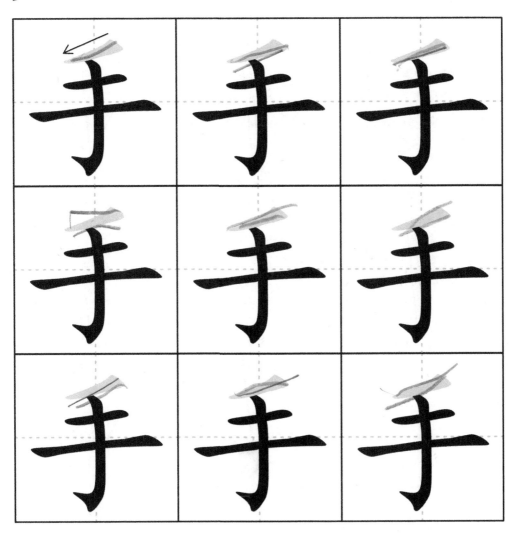

 piě

直撇

straight falling
zhí piě

 Use your finger to trace the zhí piě.

🖍 Use a pencil to trace each zhí piě ⟍.

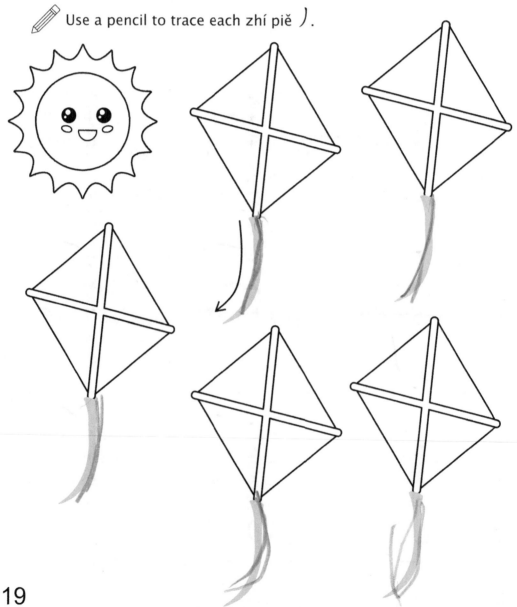

19

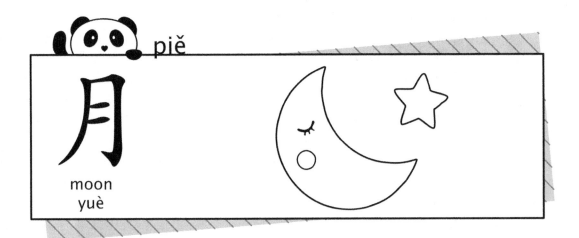

piě

月

moon
yuè

✏️ Use a pencil to trace each zhí piě).

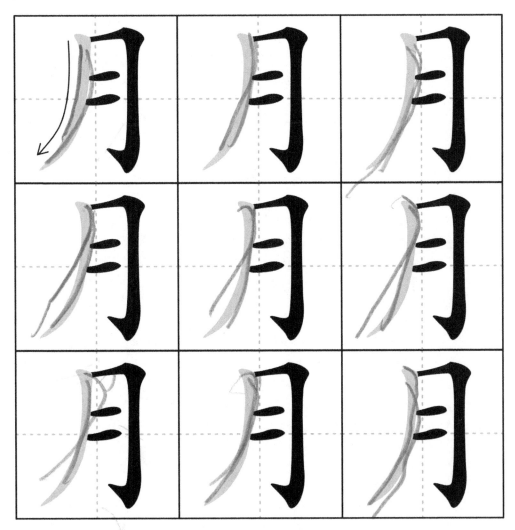

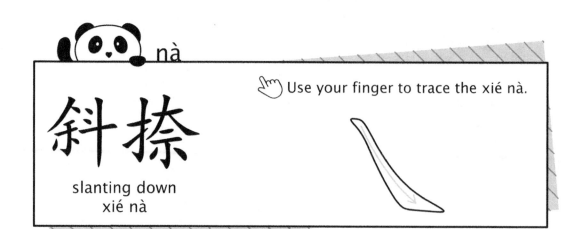

斜捺

slanting down
xié nà

Use your finger to trace the xié nà.

Use a pencil to trace each xié nà ╲ .

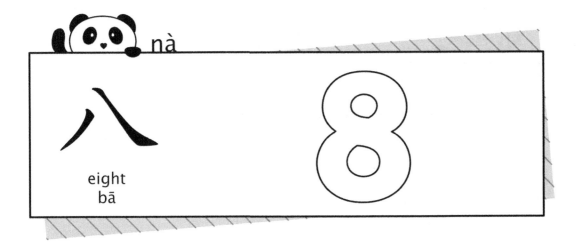

八

eight
bā

8

✏ Use a pencil to trace each xié nà ╲.

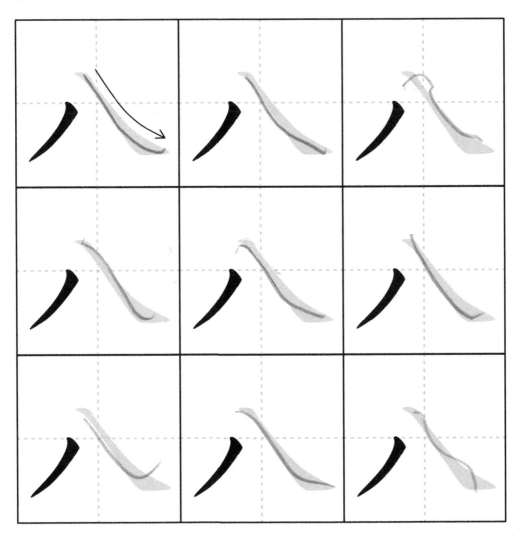

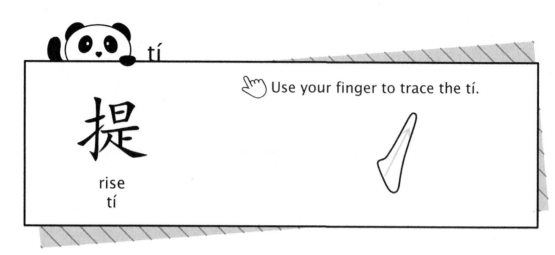

tí

提

rise
tí

👆 Use your finger to trace the tí.

✏️ Use a pencil to trace each tí ✓ .

23

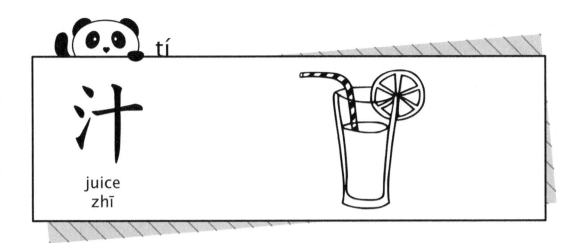

汁

juice
zhī

 Use a pencil to trace each tí ✓ .

横钩

 Use your finger to trace the héng gōu.

horizontal hook
héng gōu

 Use a pencil to trace each héng gōu ➔.

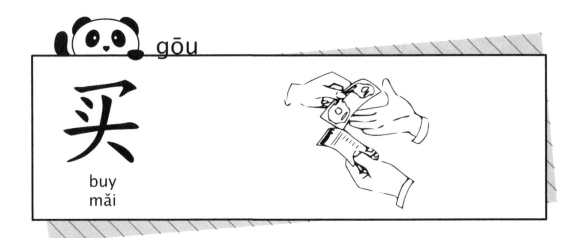

gōu

买

buy
mǎi

🖉 Use a pencil to trace each héng gōu ➔.

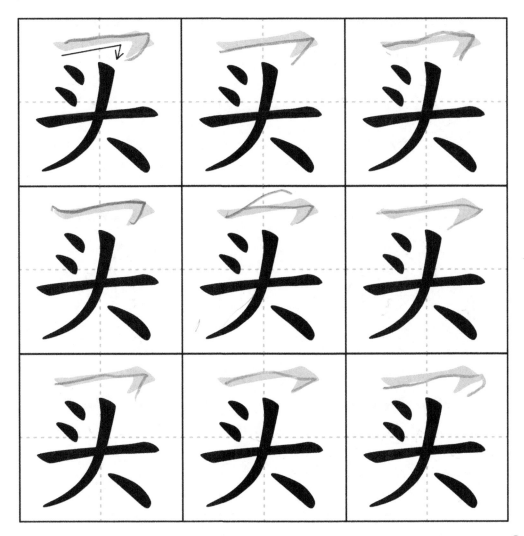

竖钩

vertical hook
shù gōu

 Use your finger to trace the shù gōu.

✏ Use a pencil to trace each shù gōu ⌡ .

27

gōu

对

correct/right
duì

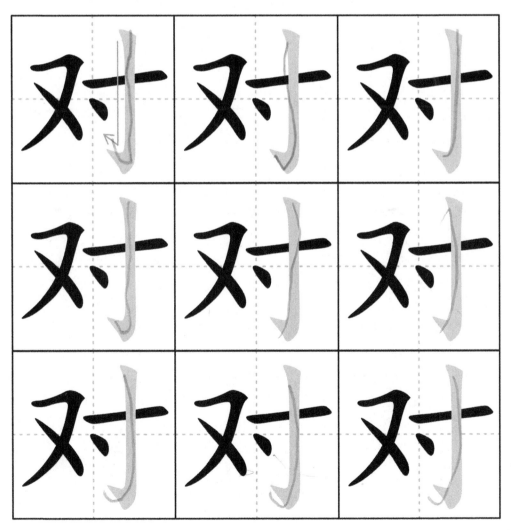

🖉 Use a pencil to trace each shù gōu 亅 .

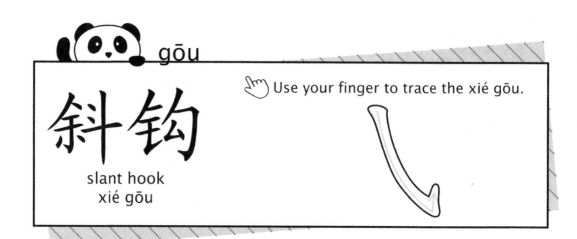

gōu

斜钩

slant hook
xié gōu

Use your finger to trace the xié gōu.

Use a pencil to trace each xié gōu .

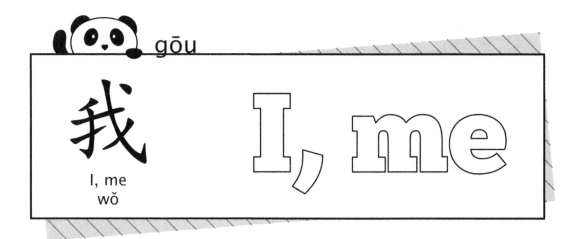

gōu

我

I, me
wǒ

I, me

 Use a pencil to trace each xié gōu ⟍ .

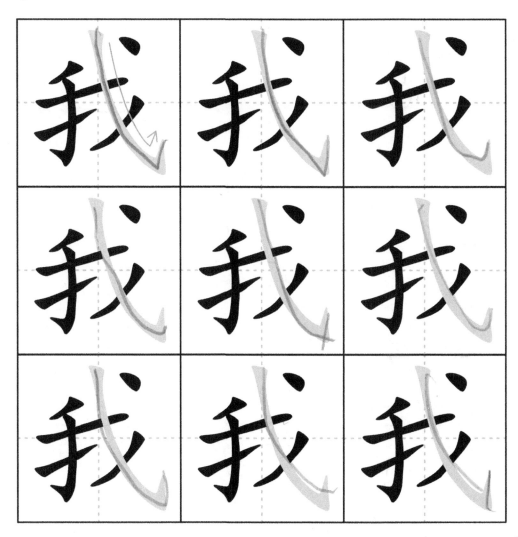

 zhé

横折

horizontal break
héng zhé

Use your finger to trace the héng zhé.

 Use a pencil to trace each héng zhé ㇕.

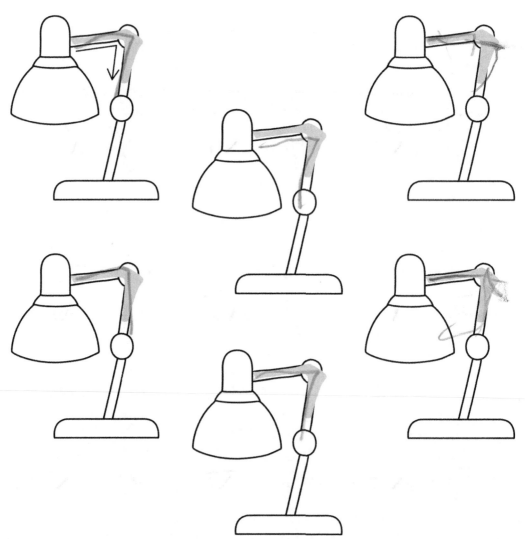

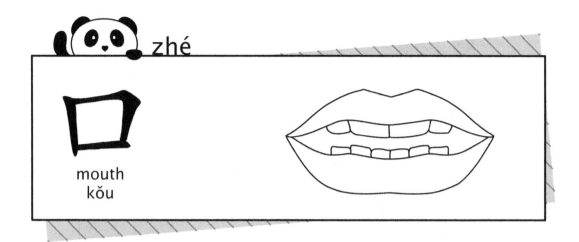

zhé

mouth
kǒu

 Use a pencil to trace each héng zhé ㄱ .

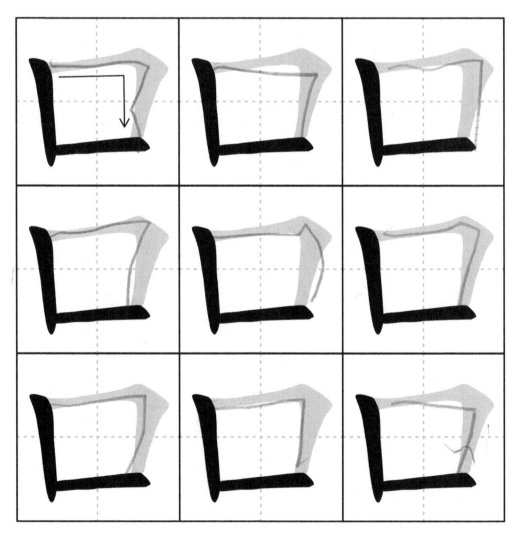

 zhé

竖折

vertical break
shù zhé

 Use your finger to trace the shù zhé.

✏️ Use your pencil to trace each shù zhé ∟.

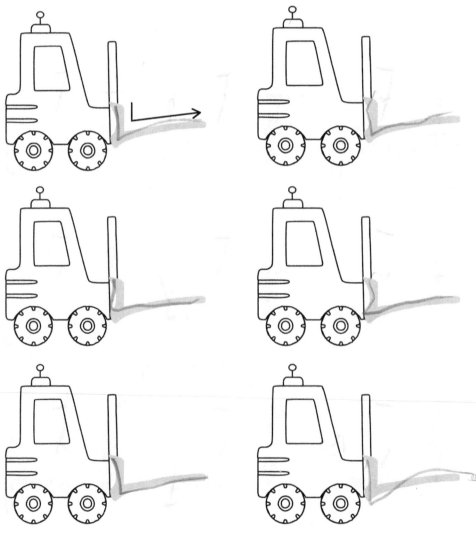

33

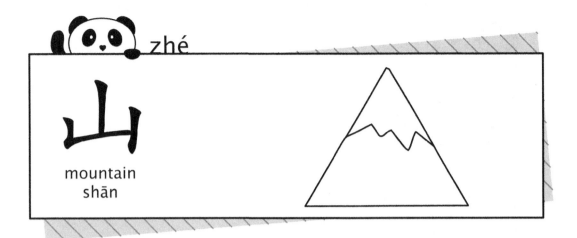

zhé

mountain
shān

 Use your pencil to trace each shù zhé ∟ .

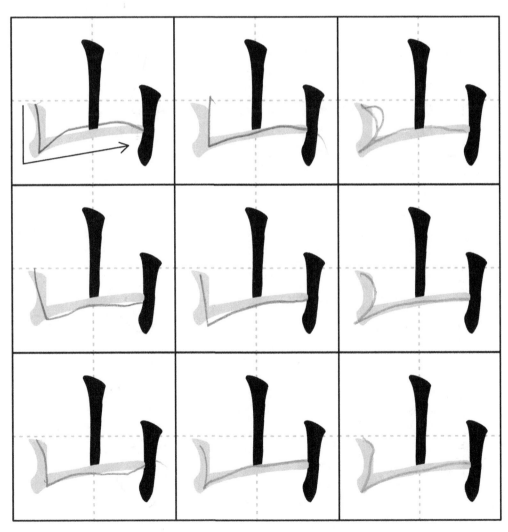

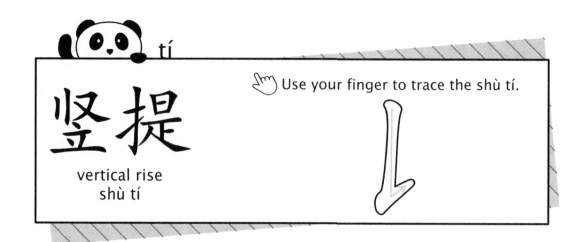

竖提

vertical rise
shù tí

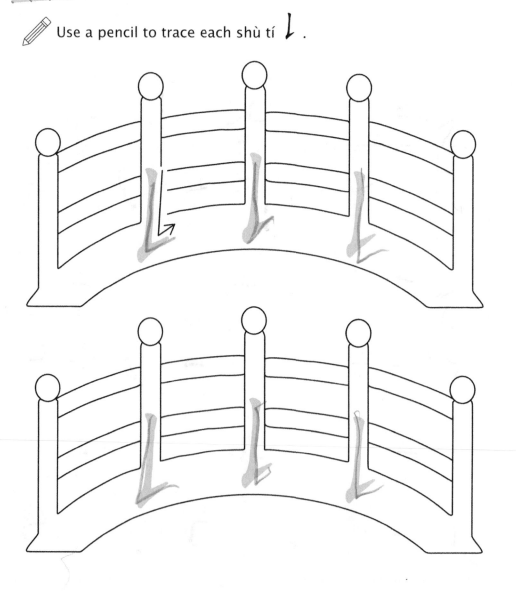

Use your finger to trace the shù tí.

Use a pencil to trace each shù tí ⌊.

35

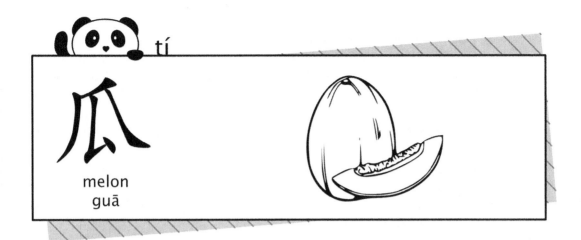

tí

瓜

melon
guā

✏ Use a pencil to trace each shù tí ↓ .

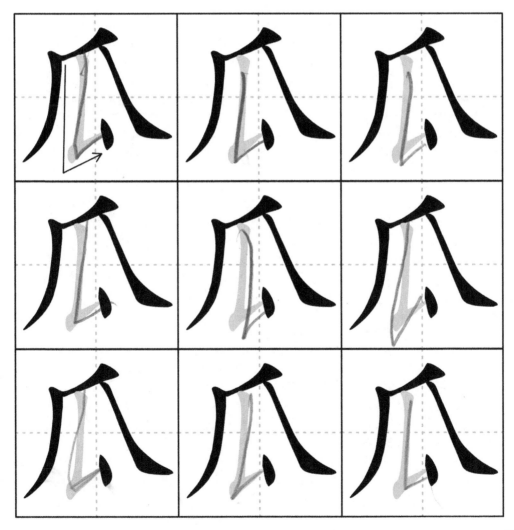

 piě

撇折

throw away break
piě zhé

 Use your finger to trace the piě zhé.

 Use a pencil to trace each piě zhé ∠.

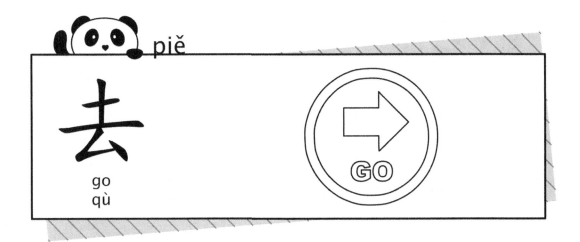

piě

去

go
qù

✏️ Use a pencil to trace each piě zhé ∠ .

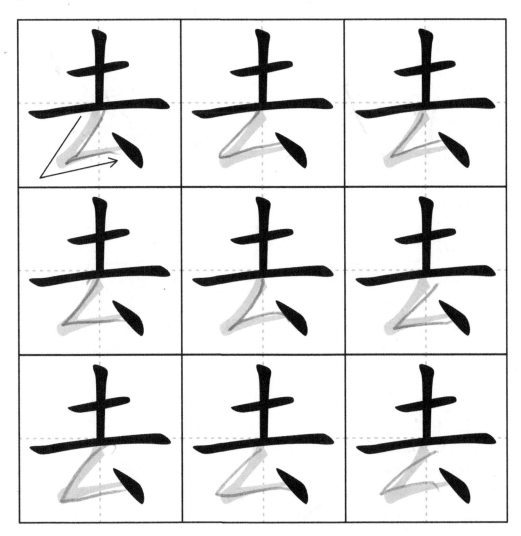

 piě

撇折

left falling dot
piě diǎn

Use a pencil to trace each piě diǎn ⟨ .

39

piě

女
female
nǚ

✏️ Use a pencil to trace each piě diǎn ㇛ .

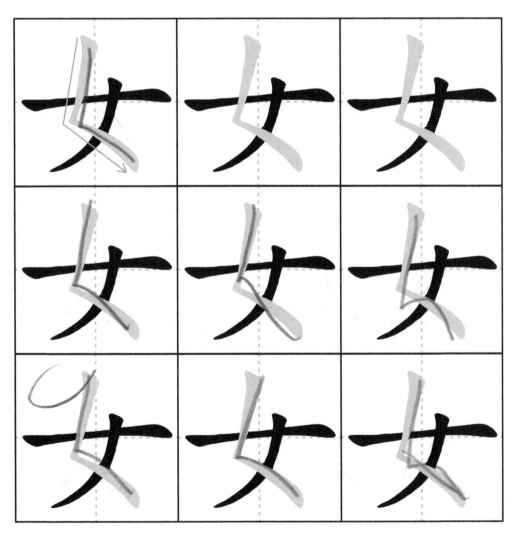

 héng piě

横撇

horizontal left falling
héng piě

👆 Use your finger to trace the héng piě.

✏️ Use a pencil to trace each héng piě 丿.

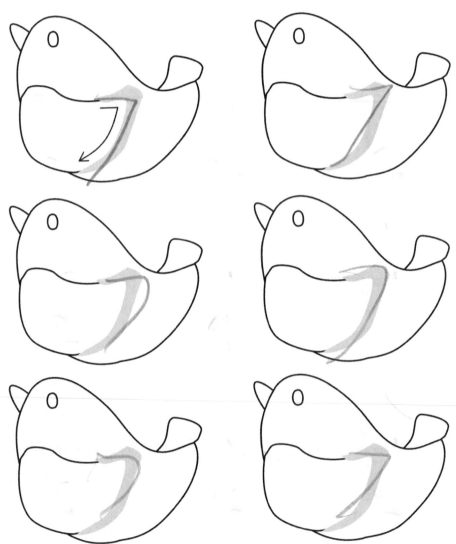

 41

冬

winter
dōng

Use a pencil to trace each héng piě 𠃌.

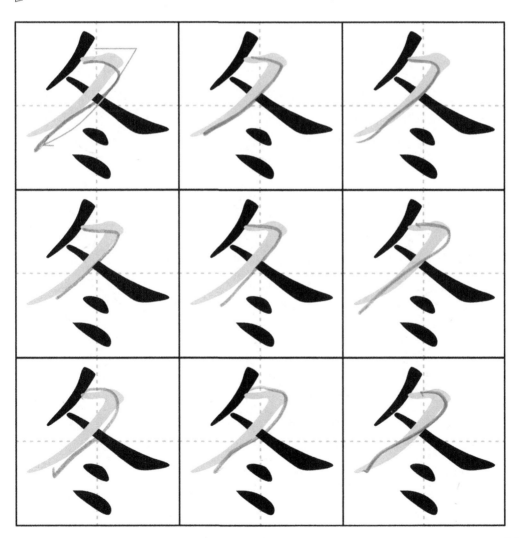

 gōu

弯钩

curve hook
wān gōu

 Use your finger to trace the wān gōu.

Use a pencil to trace each wān gōu .

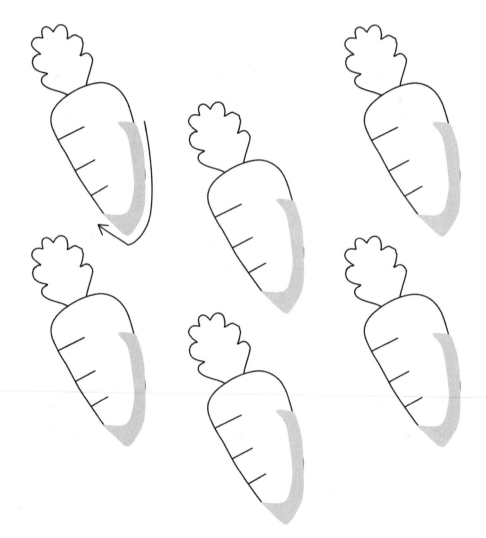

43

子

child
zi

✏️ Use a pencil to trace each wān gōu) .

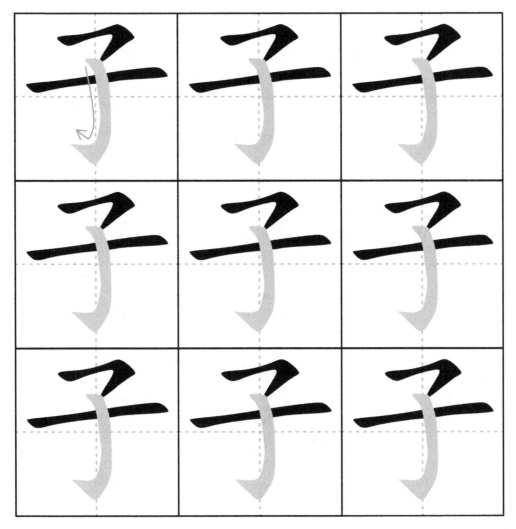

 gōu

Use your finger to trace the biǎn xié gōu.

扁斜钩

laying hook
biǎn xié gōu

 Use a pencil to trace each biǎn xié gōu  .

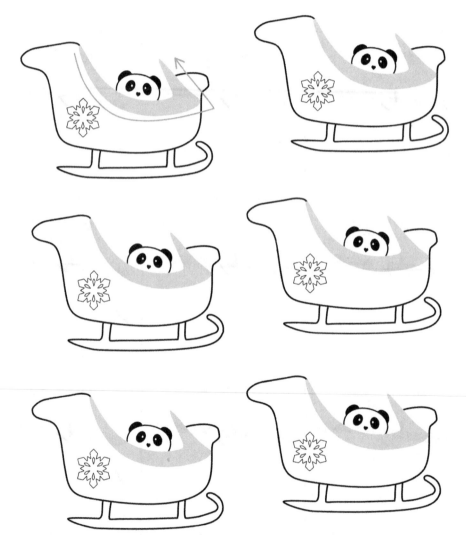

gōu

heart
xīn

✏️ Use a pencil to trace each biǎn xié gōu ↘ .

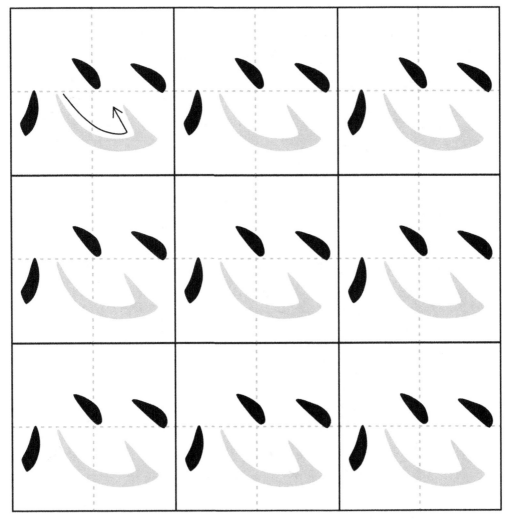

héng

Use your finger to trace the héng zhé wān gōu.

横折弯钩

horizontal break bend hook
héng zhé wān gōu

 Use a pencil to trace each héng zhé wān gōu 乙 .

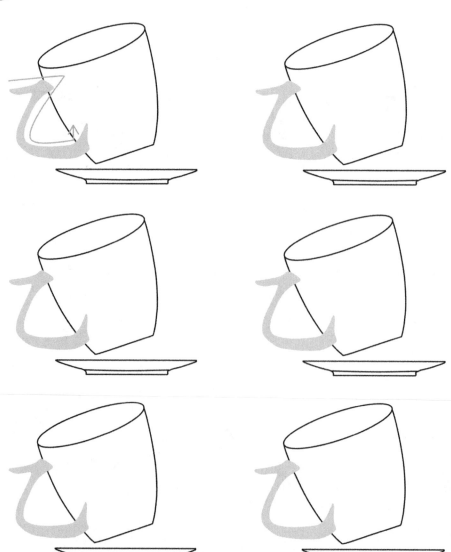

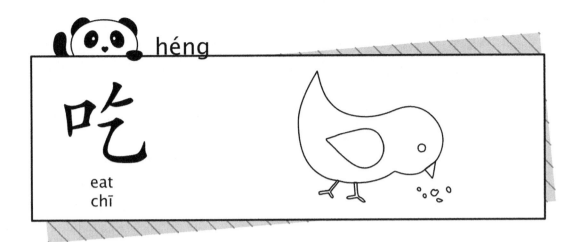

吃
eat
chī

✏️ Use a pencil to trace each héng zhé wān gōu 乙 .

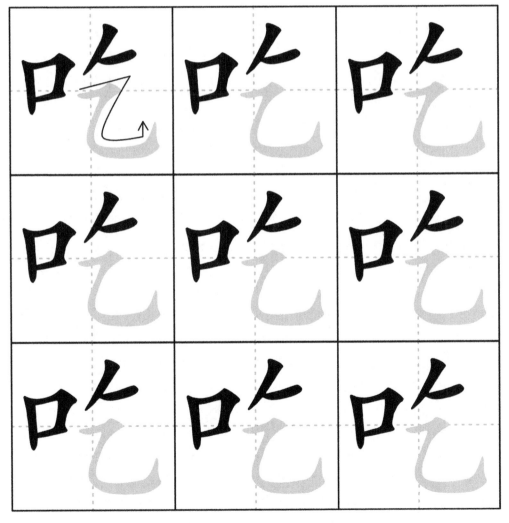

 **héng**

横斜弯钩

horizontal slant bend hook
héng xié wān gōu

 Use your finger to trace the héng xié wān gōu.

 Use a pencil to trace each héng xié wān gōu ㇈.

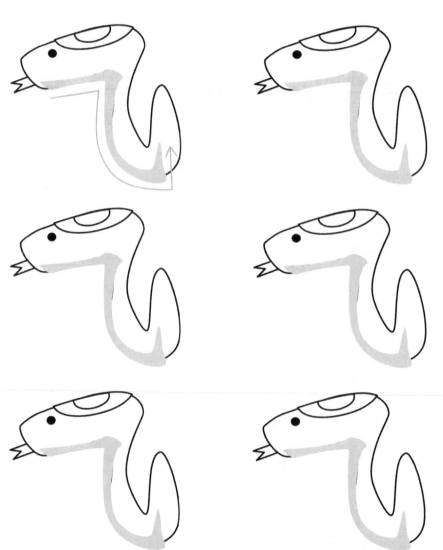

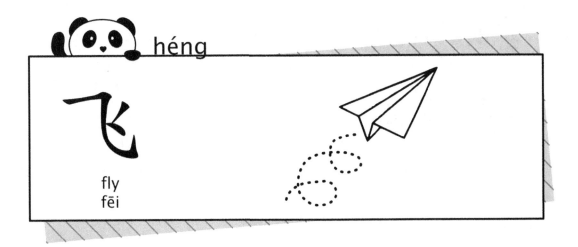

fly
fēi

✏️ Use a pencil to trace each héng xié wān gōu 乁.

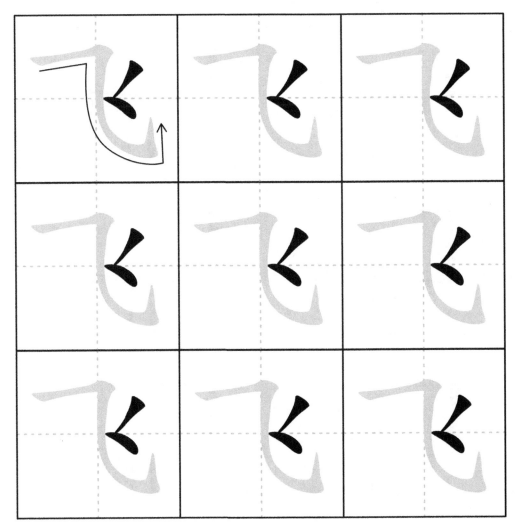

 héng

横折钩

horizontal break hook
héng zhé gōu

 Use your finger to trace the héng zhé gōu.

 Use a pencil to trace each héng zhé gōu 　.

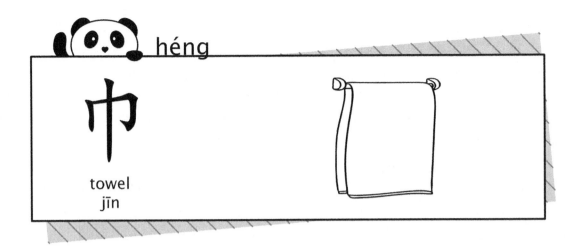

héng

巾

towel
jīn

 Use a pencil to trace each héng zhé gōu 乛.

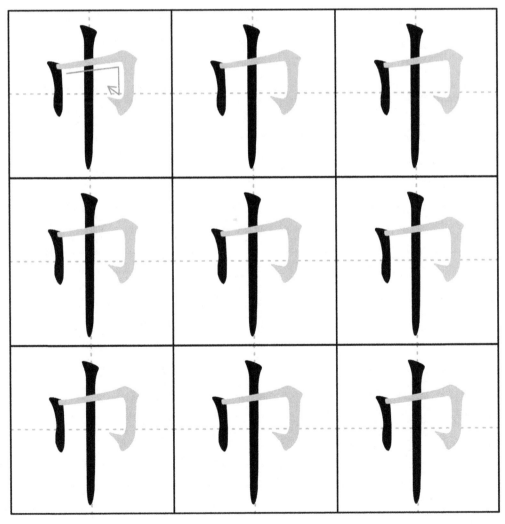

 shù

竖折弯钩

vertical break bend hook
shù zhé wān gōu

 Use your finger to trace the shù zhé wān gōu.

 Use a pencil to trace each shù zhé wān gōu 勹.

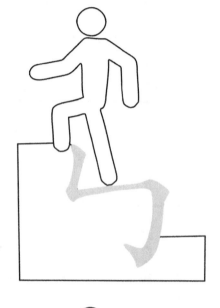

53

shù

马

horse
mǎ

 Use a pencil to trace each shù zhé wān gōu 乙 .

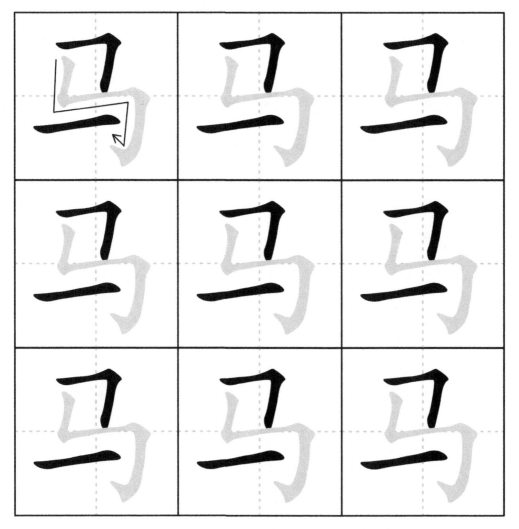

 **gōu**

竖弯钩

vertical bend hook
shù wān gōu

Use your finger to trace the shù wān gōu.

Use a pencil to trace each shù wān gōu 乚.

55

龙

dragon
lóng

✏️ Use a pencil to trace each shù wān gōu ㇄ .

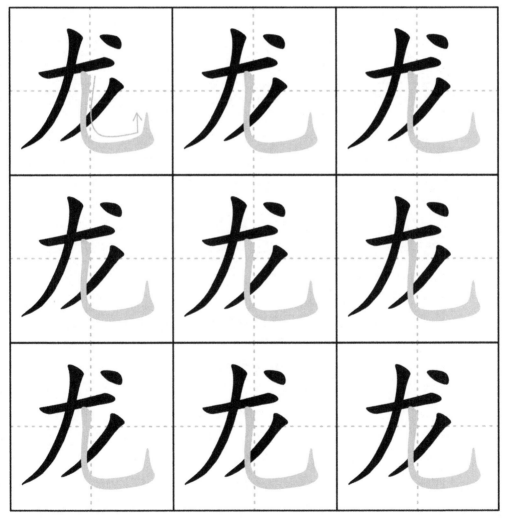

 Find and color the word 字.

WORD

WORD

WORD

字

word

zì

57

字

word
zì

WORD

 Use a pencil to trace each stroke for 字 (word).

 Find and color the word 头 .

head

tóu

头

head
tóu

✏️ Use a pencil to trace each stroke for 头 (head).

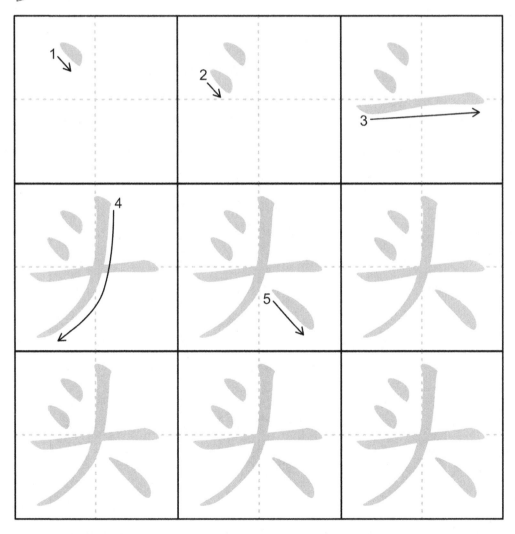

Find and color the word 二 .

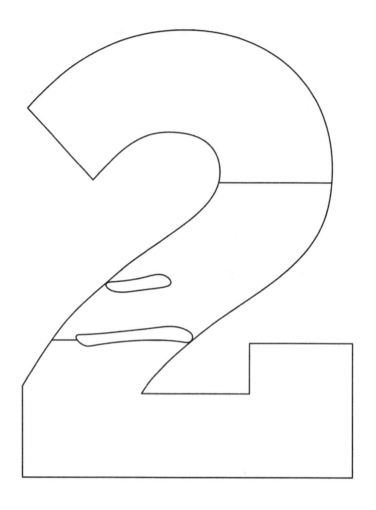

two

èr

two
èr

✏ Use a pencil to trace each stroke for 二 (two).

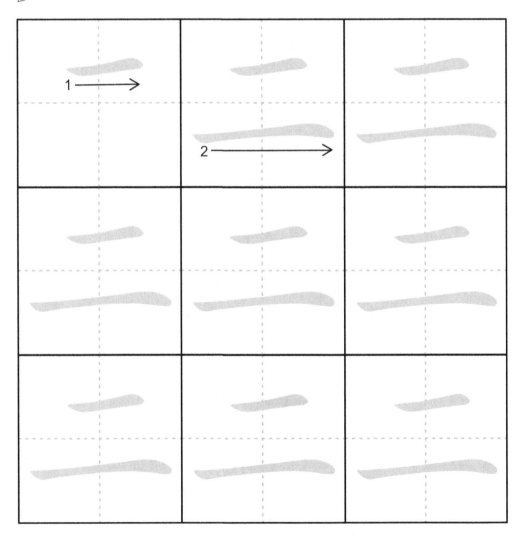

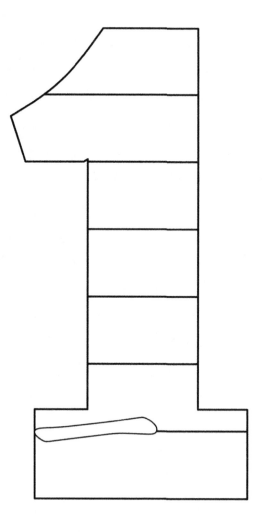

one
yī

one
yī

✏️ Use a pencil to trace each stroke for ── (one).

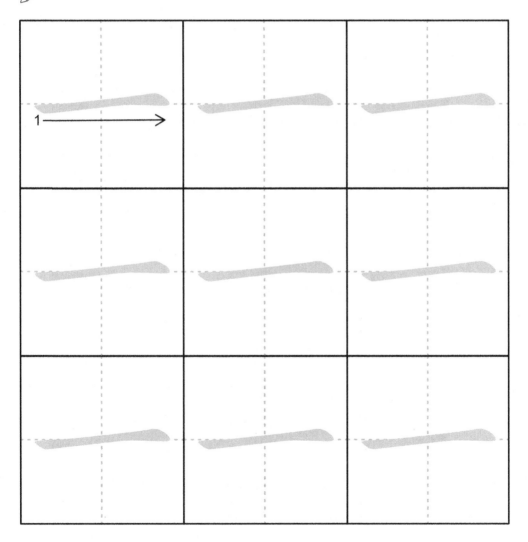

 Find and color the word 工 .

工
work
gōng

65

工

work
gōng

 Use a pencil to trace each stroke for 工 (work).

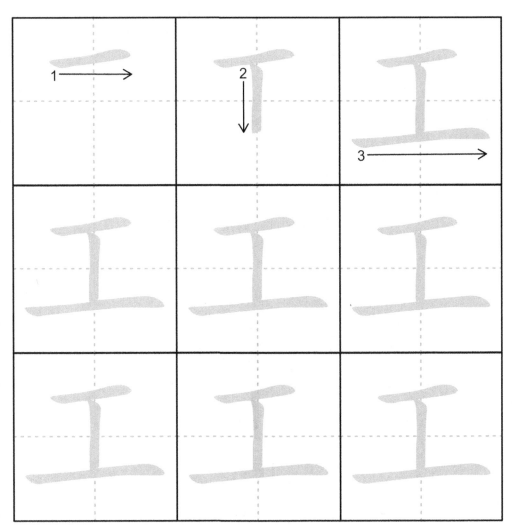

Find and color the word 十.

十

ten

shí

ten
shí

✏️ Use a pencil to trace each stroke for 十 (ten).

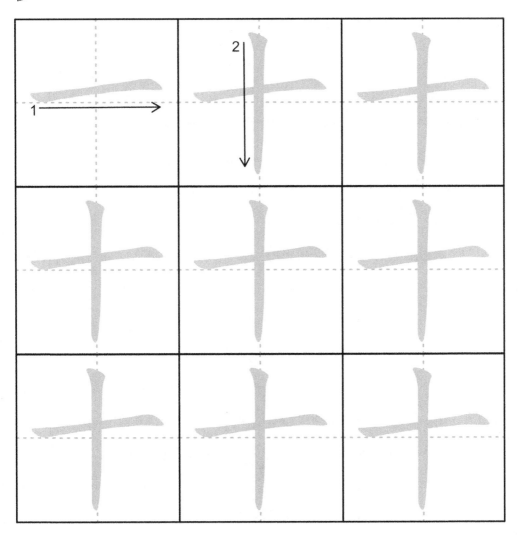

 Find and color the word 刀.

刀
knife
dāo

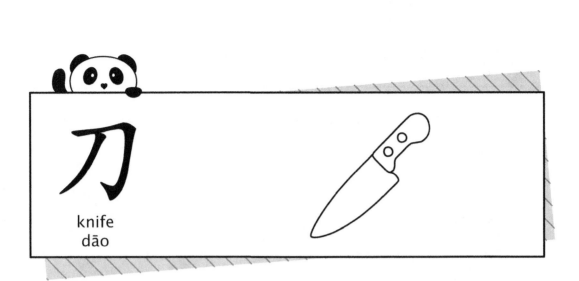

刀

knife
dāo

 Use a pencil to trace each stroke for 刀 (knife).

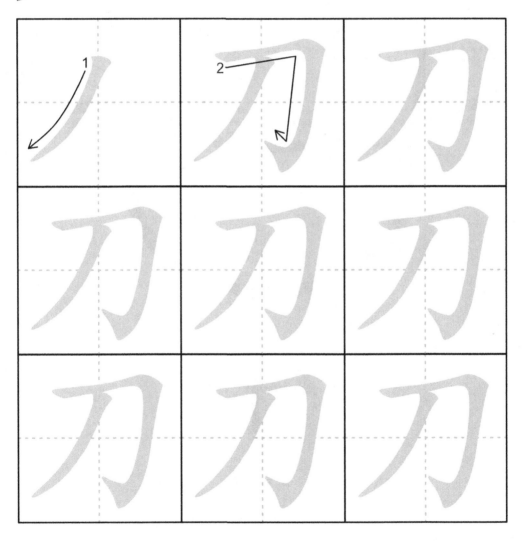

Find and color the word 牛.

牛

cow

niú

牛

cow
niú

✏️ Use a pencil to trace each stroke for 牛 (cow).

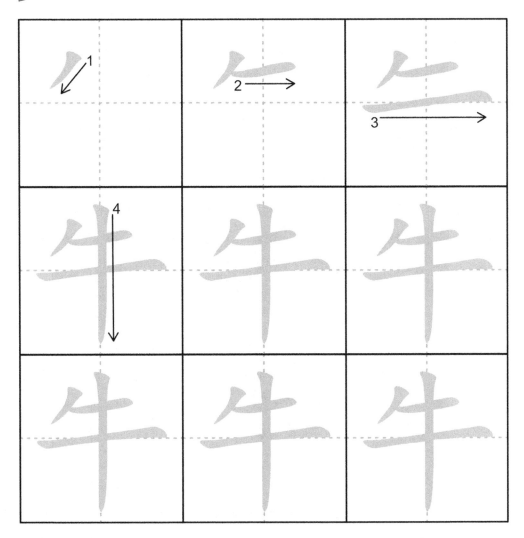

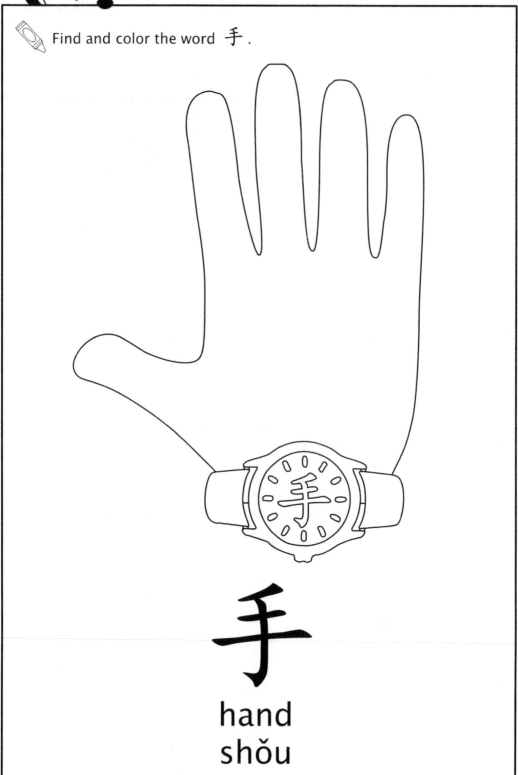

Find and color the word 手.

手
hand
shǒu

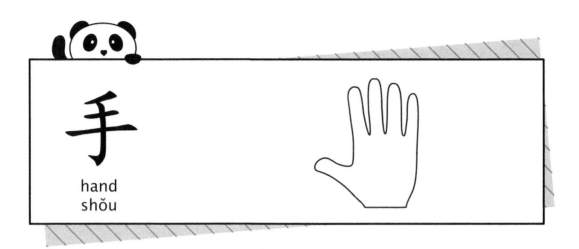

手

hand
shǒu

✎ Use a pencil to trace each stroke for 手 (hand).

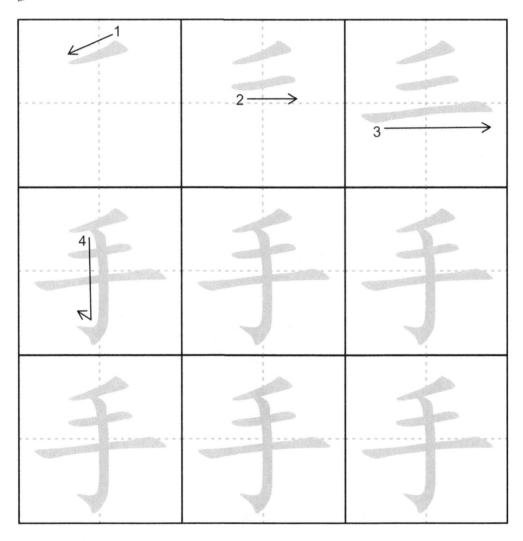

 Find and color the word 月 .

月
moon
yuè

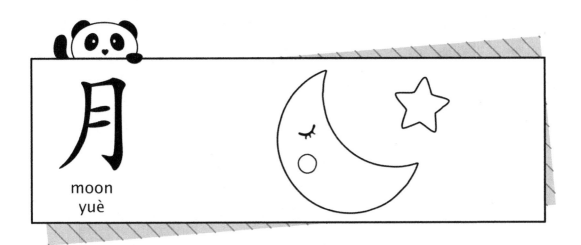

月

moon
yuè

✏️ Use a pencil to trace each stroke for 月 (moon).

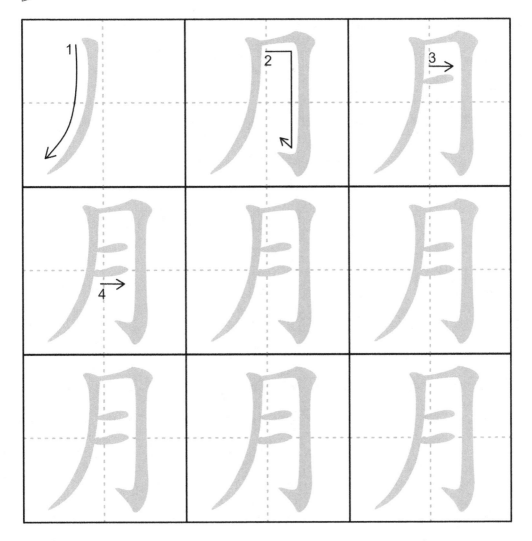

Find and color the word 八.

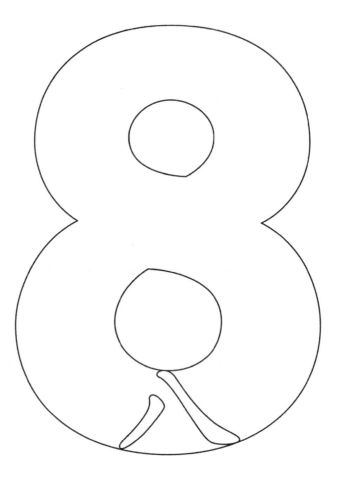

eight
bā

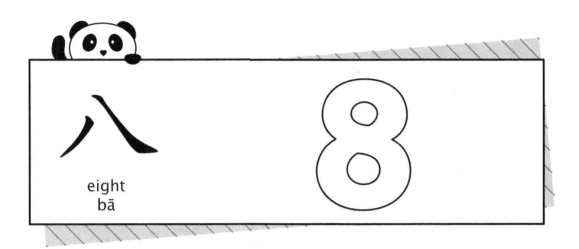

八

eight
bā

 Use a pencil to trace each stroke for 八 (eight).

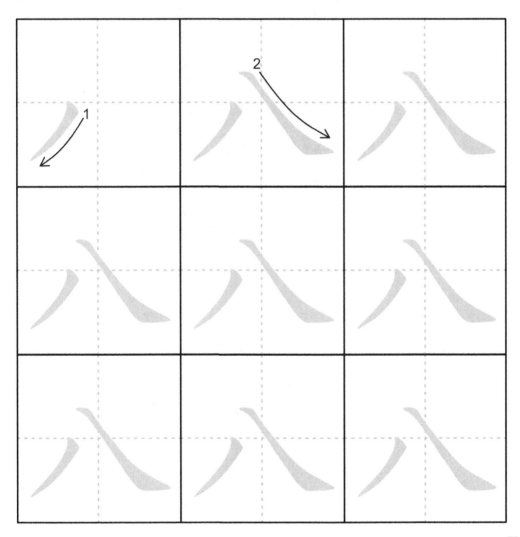

 Find and color the word 汁.

汁

juice

zhī

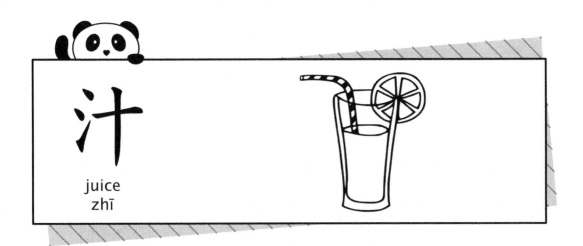

汁

juice
zhī

✏️ Use a pencil to trace each stroke for 汁 (juice).

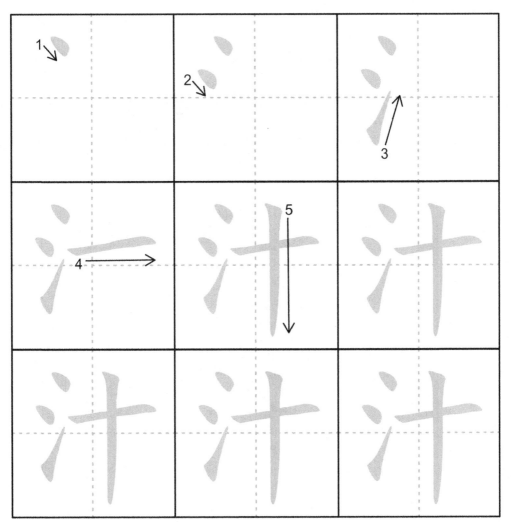

Find and color the word 买 .

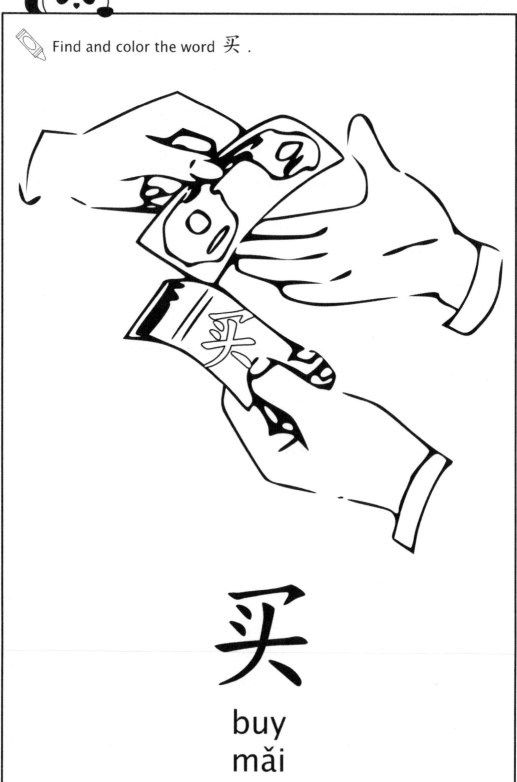

买
buy
mǎi

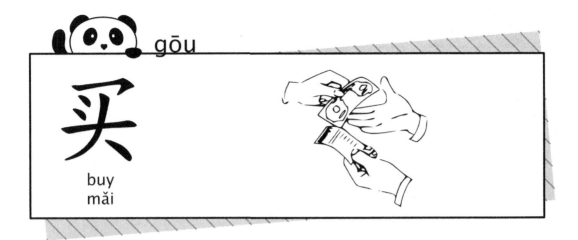

gōu

买

buy
mǎi

 Use a pencil to trace each stroke for 买 (buy).

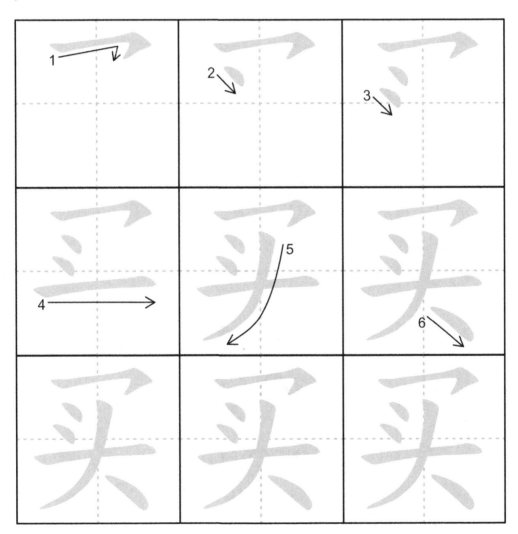

Find and color the word 对 .

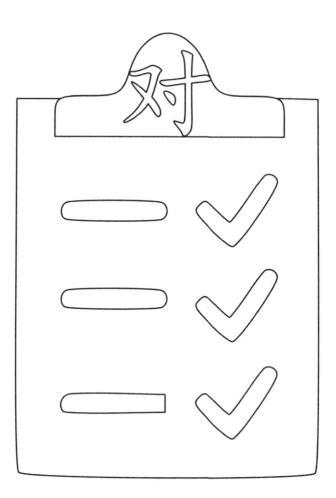

correct/right
duì

对

correct/right
duì

 Use a pencil to trace each stroke for 对 (correct/right).

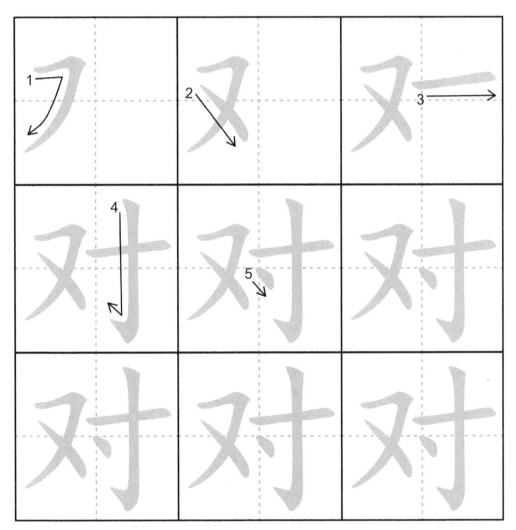

✏️ **Find and color the word 我 .**

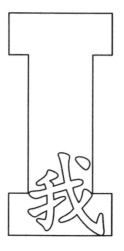

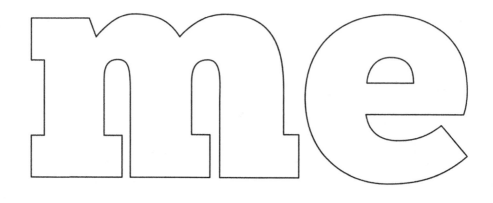

I, me

wǒ

我

I, me
wǒ

✏️ Use a pencil to trace each stroke for 我 (I, me).

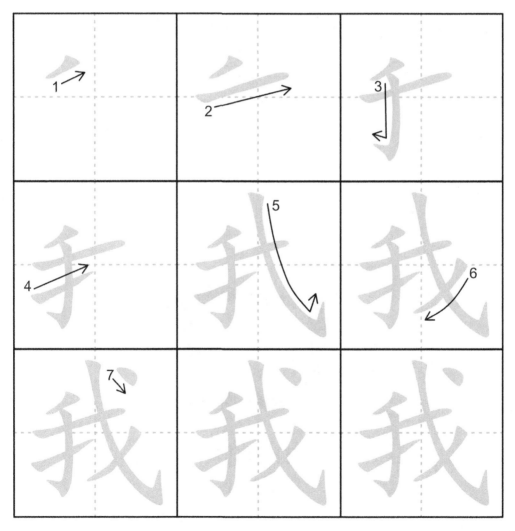

✏️ Find and color the word 口 .

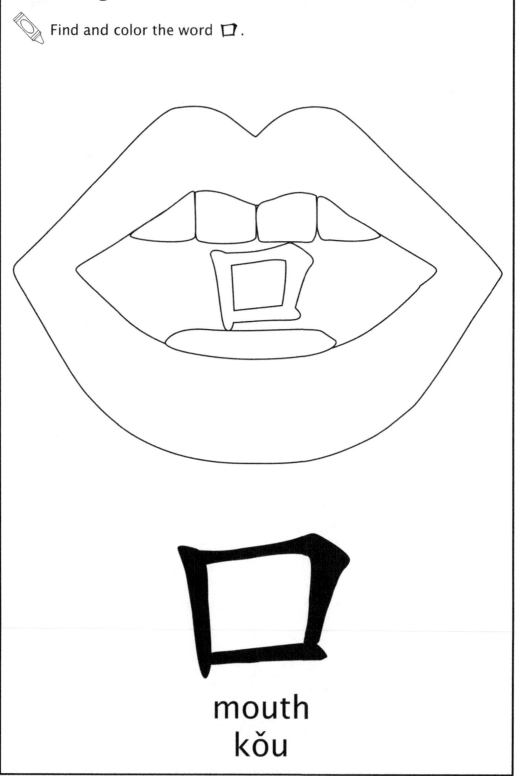

mouth
kǒu

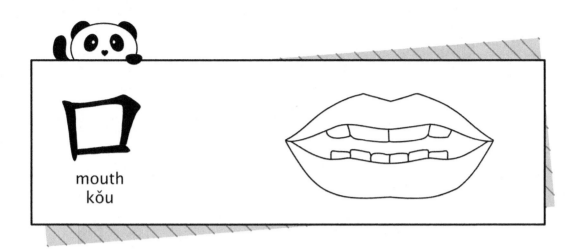

mouth
kǒu

Use a pencil to trace each stroke for 口 (mouth).

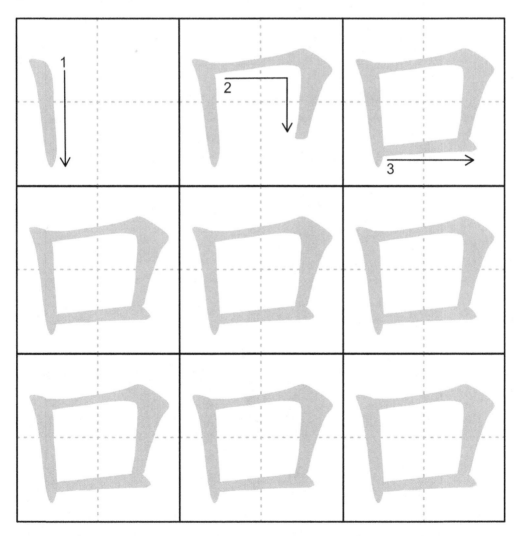

 Find and color the word 山 .

山

mountain

shān

89

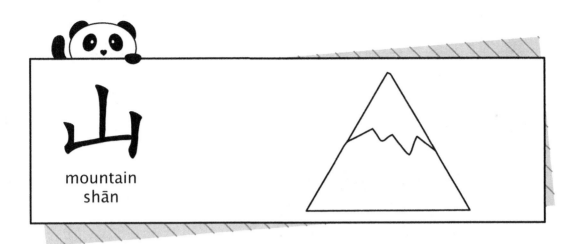

山

mountain
shān

✏️ Use your pencil to trace each stroke for 山 (mountain).

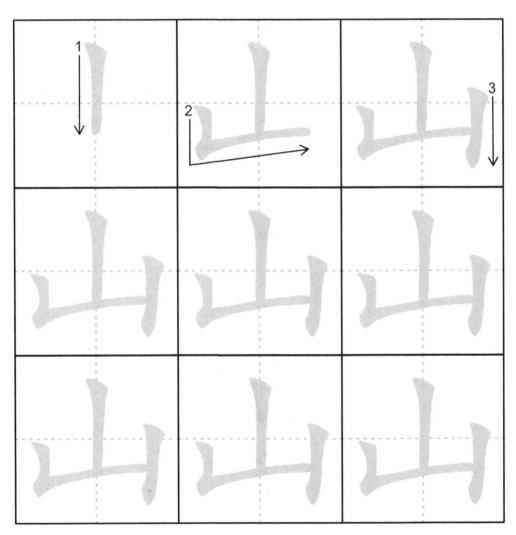

 Find and color the word 瓜 .

瓜

melon

guā

瓜

melon
guā

✏️ Use a pencil to trace each stroke for 瓜 (melon).

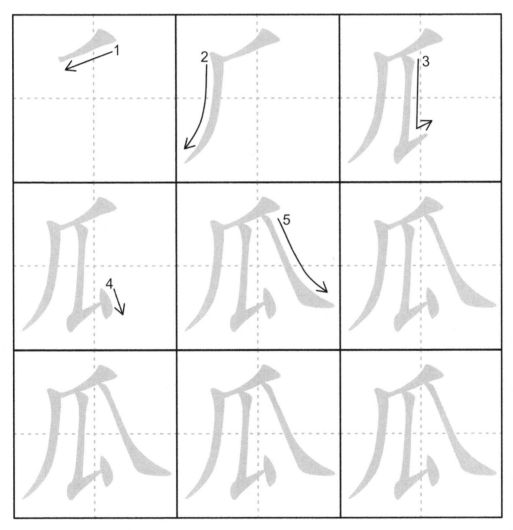

 Find and color the word 去 .

go

qù

93

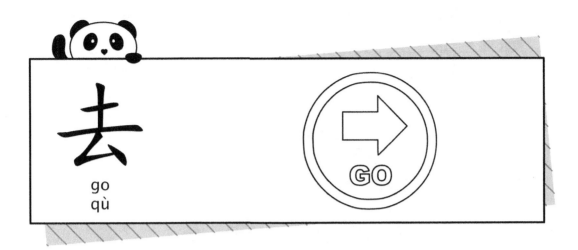

去

go
qù

✏️ Use a pencil to trace each stroke for 去 (go).

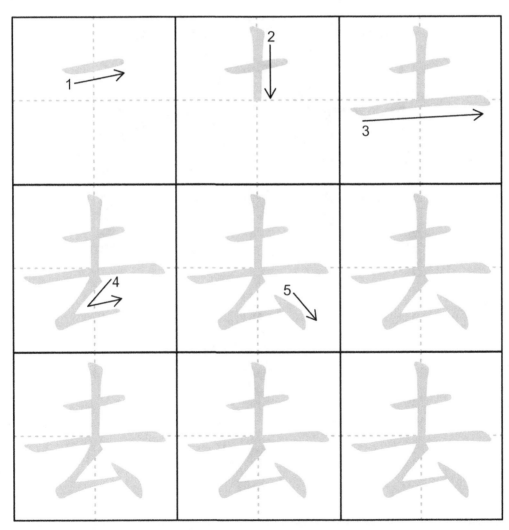

 Find and color the word 女 .

女

female

nǚ

女

female
nǔ

✏️ Use a pencil to trace each stroke for 女 (female).

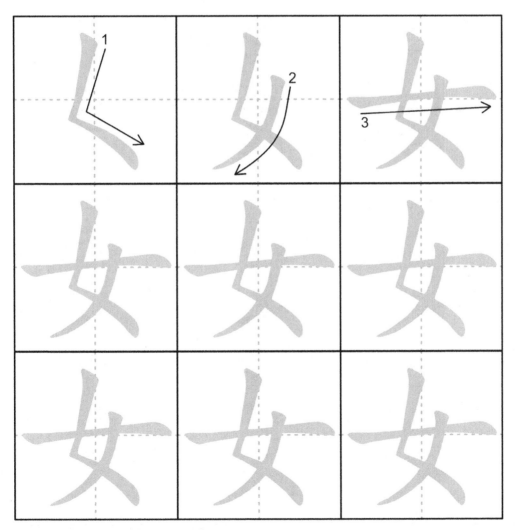

 Find and color the word 冬.

冬

winter

dōng

冬

winter
dōng

 Use a pencil to trace each stroke for 冬 (cold).

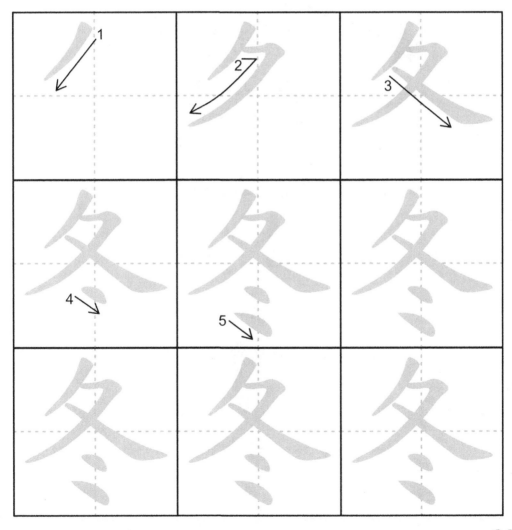

 Find and color the word 子.

子

child

zi

子

child
zi

✏️ Use a pencil to trace each stroke for 子 (child).

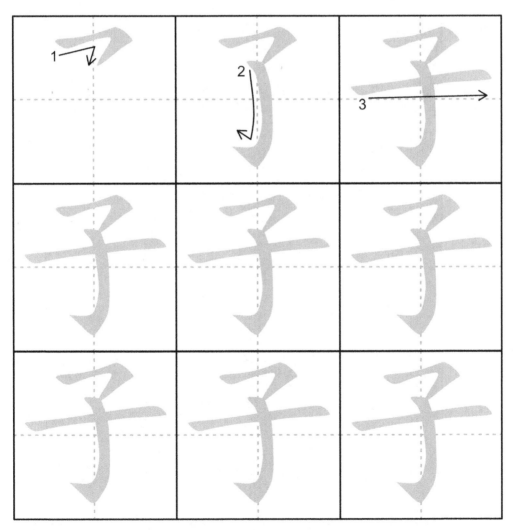

 Find and color the word 心.

heart
xīn

heart
xīn

 Use a pencil to trace each stroke for 心 (heart).

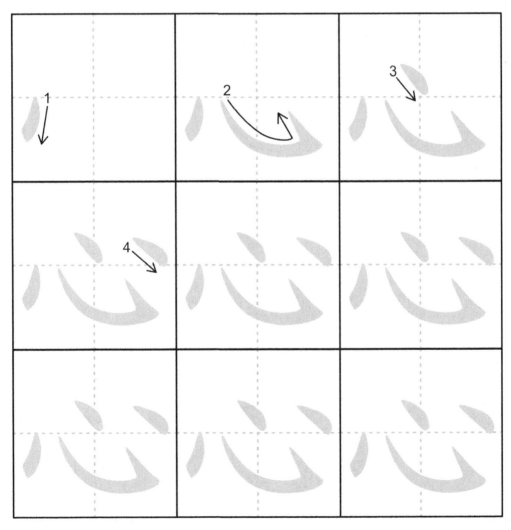

 Find and color the word 吃.

吃

eat

chī

吃

eat
chī

🖊 Use a pencil to trace each stroke for 吃 (eat).

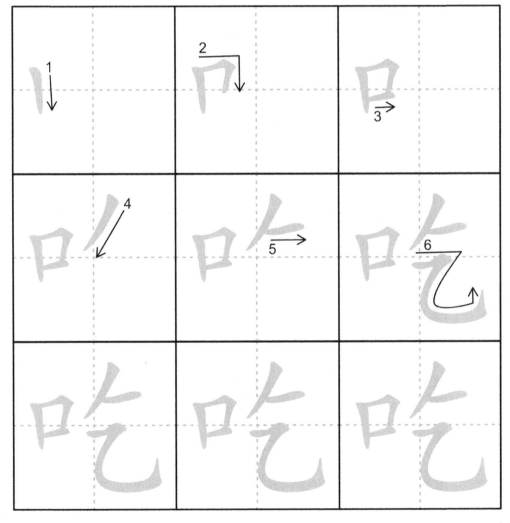

Find and color the word 飞 .

飞

fly
fēi

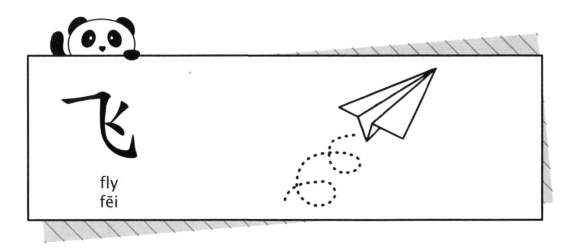

fly
fēi

 Use a pencil to trace each stroke for 飞 (fly).

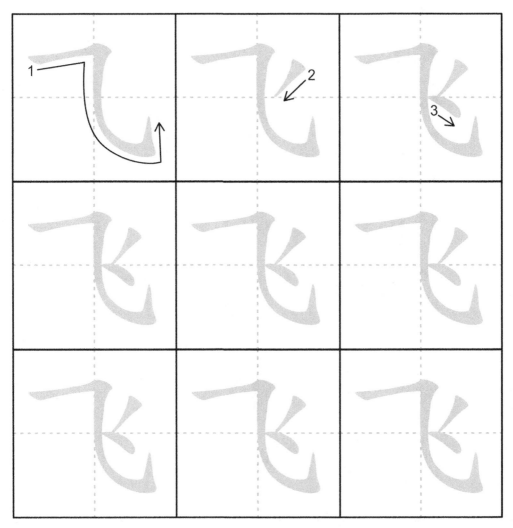

 Find and color the word 巾 .

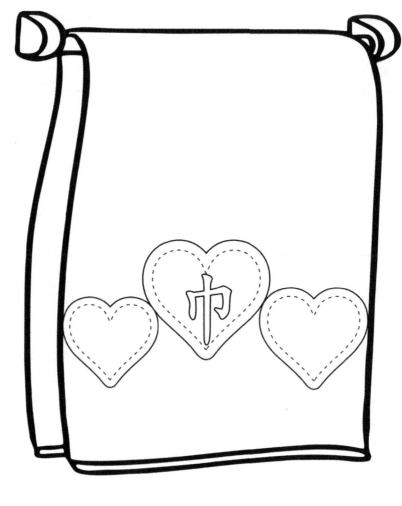

巾
towel
jīn

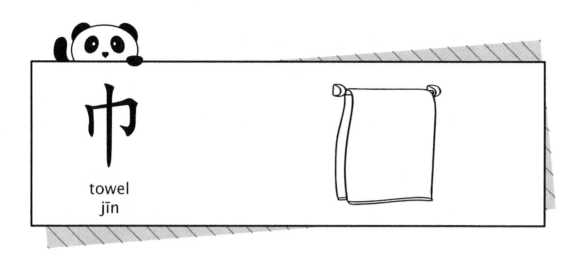

towel
jīn

 Use a pencil to trace each stroke for 巾 (towel).

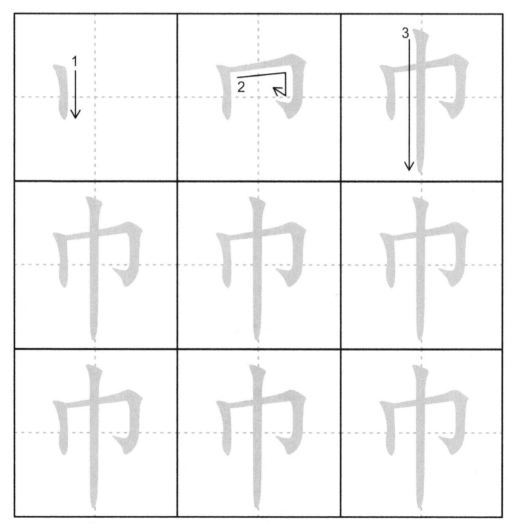

 Find and color the word 马 .

马
horse
mǎ

马

horse
mǎ

 Use a pencil to trace each stroke for 马 (horse).

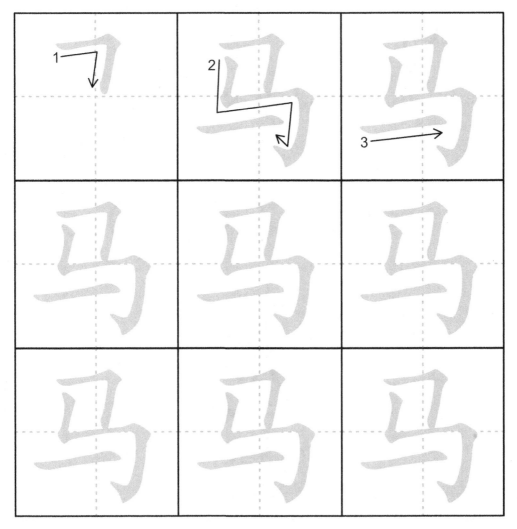

龙

dragon

lóng

龙

dragon
lóng

 Use a pencil to trace each for 龙 (dragon).

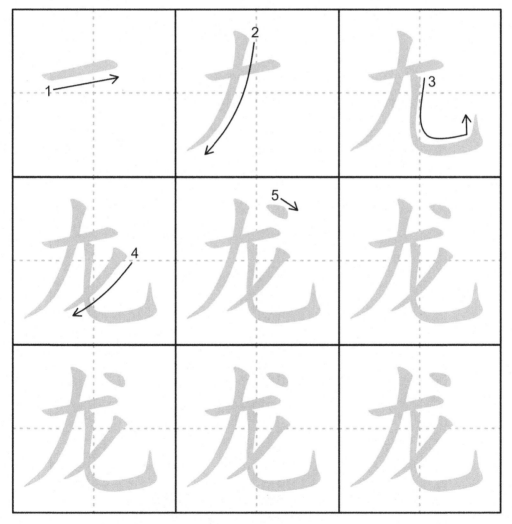

Printed in Great Britain
by Amazon

22899749R00064